Black History Activity and Enrichment Handbook

An Easy-to-use Collection of Ideas, Activities & Games Designed to Help Explore African-American History and Culture

by the editors of Just Us Books*

Executive Editors:	**Wade Hudson**
	Cheryl Willis Hudson
Senior Editor:	**Veronica Freeman Ellis**
Contributors:	**Vernell Copeland Farrand**
	Brent Farrand

Cover Design:	Culverson Blair
Book Design:	Cheryl Willis Hudson
Typography:	TrejoProduction
Illustrations:	George Ford, pp. 11, 13, 20, 21, taken from *Afro-Bets First Book About Africa: An Introduction for Young Readers* Reproduced by permission.

Special thanks to Lynn Roberts, Sandy deShield and Rosemary Jackson for reviewing the manuscript and for providing helpful comments.

Table of Contents

Introduction

Black History Month, initially Negro History Week, began as an effort by Carter G. Woodson to recognize the valuable contributions African Americans have made in the United States and throughout the world. Woodson hoped African-American history, virtually ignored, would eventually be given its just recognition as an integral part of world history.

Over six decades have passed since the first observance of Negro History Week; and yet, it is as necessary as it ever was because African-American history still has not been truly integrated into school curriculum and American life. Thus, Mr. Woodson's goal remains a challenge for us all.

This *Black History Activity and Enrichment Handbook* has been designed and created to further the work of Carter G. Woodson and others like him who have worked tirelessly to present a fair picture of the role African-Americans have played in the history of the world.

What This Book Is

This handbook is foremost a guide to activities and inquiries which are designed to enhance knowledge of African-American history and culture.

- It is a handbook which spotlights several key themes in this area of study.
- It is a ready resource book of support materials for these selected themes.
- It is a tool for approaching the celebration of African-American history in an active and participatory way. Both children and adults can experience these activities together.
- It is a short entry handbook designed to stimulate discussion, communication and action, ultimately adding to the fabric of knowledge concerning African-American history and culture.

What This Book Is Not

This handbook is *not* a teacher's guide for a specific textbook. Some activities suggested have been based on general information provided in *Afro-Bets Book of Black Heroes* and *Afro-Bets First Book About Africa*. However, many other resources are recommended to provide more specific, in-depth coverage of various topics.

- It is *not* a curriculum guide to African-American Studies. Our purpose is to engage attention and provide motivation for further study. The handbook is, however, easily adaptable to lesson plans and instructional objectives required in classroom teaching. It is also intended to be "user friendly" for parents, church groups, and community organizations. Creative users will adapt the activities for all age groups as well.

- It is *not* a comprehensive activity guide or an academic text. It is meant to be a point of departure—an invitation to the reader to gather a basic core of facts and then through critical thinking and a hands-on approach,to extract knowledge through analysis, application and evaluation.

- Our intent is *not* to add to the learner's mind more fragments of facts, but rather to suggest activities that will weave a tapestry of knowledge.

A Recommendation

In using this handbook, we ask that you not make any child or adult distrust his own body of experience or feel empty before the richness of the African-American heritage. This handbook is for all. We encourage you to take care to integrate each new fact, each new hero, and each new discovery into what the reader already knows and feels. We hope the journey is an exciting one.

How to Get Started

Keep the Focus: This handbook is organized thematically by identifiable guideposts in African-American History. #1 Africa–The Beginning; #2 The Middle Passage; #3 Slavery vs. Freedom; #4 The Oral Tradition; #5 Reconstruction to Civil Rights; #6 The Diaspora.

The guideposts are supported by specific activities for groups and individuals. **Read About** and **Investigate** provide additional questions and extension activities.

Creative group leaders will be able to direct numerous questions which will arise from the introduction of these topics. Keep the focus by emphasizing that it is important for a people to know their past, for only then will they be able to cope with the present and plan for the future.

Stay Organized: To achieve maximum benefits from the activities, readers should use library resources to supplement the information provided. Use a folder to keep copies of notes and additional resources that are collected. Review the materials from time to time. The bibliography included in the handbook, **Resources**, is merely a starting point. Local librarians can help in locating films, recordings, videos and other material to expand the information provided in the handbook. Talking to older people and tape recording their oral history is also a valuable resource.

Set Goals and Rewards: The importance of setting goals and establishing criteria for rewards cannot be overemphasized. If African-American history celebrations in your school or community center are limited, select one guidepost for *thorough* exploration. Or if larger blocks of time are available, set aside a regular period of time each day or each week to explore various aspects of African-American history. Reward teams or individuals for outstanding participation, efforts, or reports. Setting goals for each topic will enable readers to understand exactly what needs to be accomplished. Rewards are tangible evidence that readers have achieved the goals. Photocopies of the certificate provided at the end of this handbook may be used as such rewards. Teachers or readers may also create culminating activities, programs, or performances or their own awards.

Celebrate Your Efforts: Plan a festival or celebration for the end of Black History Month (see page 32). Use knowledge your group has gained from exploring the guideposts and related activities to create a Heritage Quilt (see pages 30–31). This quilt or wall hanging may be used as a visual centerpiece for your celebration and ideas for making it may be collected as the group follows each guidepost. If you are so inspired, continue the activities throughout the year. Now let's get started!

Find out what you already know about African-American history and culture by taking this short puzzle-quiz. Keep a note of how well you do. Then, after reading the *Handbook* and doing some of the activities suggested, take the quiz again. See how much more you have learned about the history and culture of African-Americans.

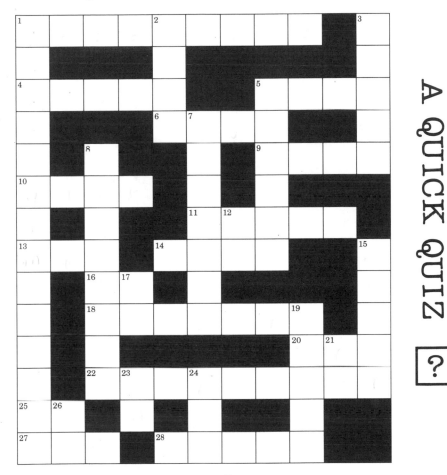

A QUICK QUIZ ?

Across

1. She refused to give up her seat on a bus. *(two words)*
4. The war that decided the fate of slaves
5. A gifted actor charged with communism
6. Martin Luther King, Jr. spoke often of this.
9. Marian Anderson used to sing this.
10. Jan Matzeliger's invention revolutionized this industry.
11. Last name of 22 across
13. Carpet
14. Langston Hughes
16. Sixth musical note
18. Cinque's mutiny took place here.
20. Plural of *is*
22. A speaker at the 1852 Women's Rights Convention in Akron, Ohio
25. Preposition
27. He led a slave revolt.
28. Denmark _____

Down

1. The period during which some southern states were under military government
2. Opposite of *push*
3. Southern city from which Martin Luther King, Jr. led a protest march
5. George Washington Carver discovered many uses for this item.
7. Martin Luther King, Jr. Malcolm X, and Jesse Jackson
8. He was once a slave.
12. In reference to
15. Actress Pam _____
17. I _____ somebody!
19. Actor _____ Glover
21. 12 down
23. 25 across
24. Number after zero
26. Not applicable

Africa—The Beginning

More than ninety percent of the evidence relating to human origin has come from the continent of Africa. Important archaeological finds have been made in Olduvai Gorge and Laetolil in Tanzania, on the shores of Lake Turkana in Kenya, and in South Africa. These and other finds in Africa suggest strongly that the world's second largest continent is the birthplace of mankind.

There are people of African descent all over the world. Some can trace their ancestry directly to Africa; others cannot. Even though people of African descent may live far from Africa, their cultures tell the world that Africa is their beginning. These people have not forgotten their African origins, and neither should you.

What Do You Know? True or False

Write the letter **T** in the space provided if the statement is true. Write the letter **F** if the statement is false.

_____ 1. Africa is the second largest continent in the world.

_____ 2. Africa has had universities only in modern times.

_____ 3. African kingdoms became less powerful because of the slave trade.

_____ 4. Africa is rich in natural resources.

_____ 5. All of Africa is still ruled by European countries.

_____ 6. Africa has many countries, but only one group of people who speak the same language.

_____ 7. It has always been easy to explore Africa's interior.

_____ 8. The East African savanna is home to animals such as lions, zebras, giraffes, and cheetahs.

_____ 9. Africans create works of art only for religious purposes.

RESOURCES

African Countries and Cultures: A Concise Illustrated Dictionary. Jane M. Hornburger, and Alex Whitney. New York: David McKay Company, Inc., 1981.

Ancient Africa. F. A. Chijioke, New York: Africana Publishing Corporation, 1971.

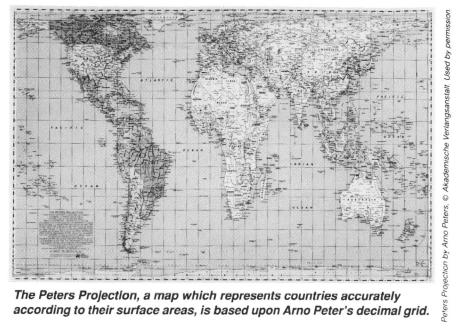

The Peters Projection, a map which represents countries accurately according to their surface areas, is based upon Arno Peter's decimal grid.

FACTS

Area: 11,694,000 sq. mi.

Population: approximately 600 million—world's third largest population
Nigeria—most populous country

Number of independent countries: 51 (as of 1989)

Highest mountain: Kilimanjaro (19,340 ft.) in Tanzania, East Africa

Longest river: Nile (4,100 miles) in Egypt—world's longest river

Largest desert: Sahara (3.5 million sq. miles)—worlds' largest desert

Languages: more than 800 languages

Religions: African traditional religions, Islam, Christianity

Climate: tropical

Economy: agriculture, mining, fishing, forestry

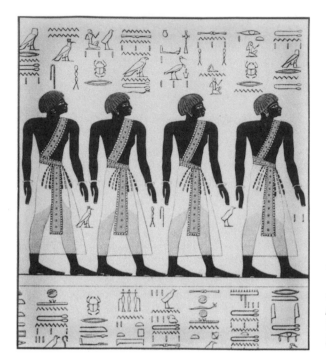

People of Kush are represented in a painting from a royal tomb located in the Valley of the Kings, Egypt. Around 1300 B.C.

Making Connections

What do Africa and America have in common? To help you answer that question, write the letters that spell **Africa** down the left side of a sheet of paper. Next to each letter, write a description of Africa that begins with the letter. Your description may be a single word or a phrase. Do the same for the letters that spell **America**. Some of your descriptions should be the same for both words. Follow the example below.

Ancient	**A**
F	**M**odern
Rich in natural resources	**E**
I	**R**ich in natural resources
C	**I**
A	**C**
	A

Activity: Getting a Sense of History

Timeline

A timeline is usually a line that shows important dates and events in history. In this activity, however, you will modify a timeline to get a sense of historical time.

Materials

- 100 foot ball of light-colored string
- measuring tape or ruler
- colored markers

Using the string, measure out one inch for each 100 years that Africa was the center of civilization (approximately 2500 years). Choose a colored marker and mark the end of that measurement.

Continuing on the same string, measure out one inch for each 100 years of European Renaissance—rebirth of learning—(approximately 300 years). Mark the end of that measurement with a different colored marker.

Still using the same string, measure two inches for the approximately 200 years of United States independence. Mark the end of that measurement with a third colored marker.

Write a brief explanation for your timeline and display it and the timeline at school or at home.

Where does chattel slavery in the United States fit into this timeline?

It is important to emphasize that study of African-American history begins with the study of African societies, before European contact on the continent. The enslavement of Africans in the Western hemisphere and the United States occurred much later.

Ancient African Kingdoms

Life in the ancient African kingdoms fascinated travelers who were fortunate to pay visits there. These travelers were especially impressed with the wealth and system of government that existed within the kingdoms.

Timbuktu in 1526

The inhabitants, and especially strangers there residing, are exceeding rich ... Here are many wells containing most sweet water; and so often as the river Niger overfloweth, they convey the water thereof by certain sluices into the town.

Corn, cattle, milk, and butter this region yeildeth in great abundance; but salt is very scarce here; for it is brought hither by land from Taghaza which is 500 miles distant ... The rich king of Timbuktu hath many plates and sceptres of gold, some whereof weight 1300 pounds; and he keeps a magnificent and well furnished court ... All his soldiers ride upon horses ... Here are great store of doctors, judges, priests and other learned men ... and hither are brought divers manuscripts or written books out of Barbary, which are sold for more money than any other merchandise.

From Leo Africanus, aka Al Hassan Ibn Muhammad, The History and Description of Africa done into English by John Pory *(London: Hakluyt Society, 1896) pp. 824–26.*

How would you have reacted to a visit with a ruler of Ghana, Mansa Musa of Mali, or the Oba of Benin? Do one of the following to show your reactions.

- Write a journal entry of a visit to one of the kingdoms.
- Write the conversation that might have taken place between you and Mansa Musa.

Investigate

- **The concept of kingship** (ancient African, western and eastern)—Make a chart to show the characteristics of kingship in ancient Africa, the West, and the East.

- **The trans-saharan gold-salt trade**—Trace a map of Africa and indicate the kingdoms of Ghana, Mali, and Songhay. Then label the route of the gold-salt trade.

- **Egyptian civilization**—Trace, draw, or cut out from magazines pictures that show examples of ancient Egyptian civilization. Use these pictures to make a collage.

Read About

The horsemen of Kanem-Bornu—Imagine that there is going to be a movie about the horsemen of Kanem-Bornu. Design a poster to advertise the movie.

The Great Temple at Great Zimbabwe—Use modeling clay to construct a model of the Great Temple.

The trading center at Kilwa—Make a list of the commodities that were traded at Kilwa. Next to each commodity, draw an item that can be made from the material.

RESOURCES

A Glorious Age in Africa. Daniel Chu and Elliott Skinner, Zenith/ Doubleday, 1965.

A History of East and Central Africa. Basil Davidson, New York: Doubleday Anchor.

A History of West Africa. Basil Davidson, New York: Doubleday Anchor.

Africa in the Days of Exploration, R. and C. Oliver, Spectrum Books. Englewood Cliffs, N.J.: Prentice-Hall, 1965.

Africa: It's Empires, Nations, and People. Mary Penick Motley, Detroit: Wayne State University Press, 1969.

Afro-Bets First Book About Africa, Veronica Freeman Ellis, Orange, N.J.: Just Us Books, 1989.

Ancient African Kingdoms. Golden Legacy Illustrated History Magazine. Dix Hills, N.Y.: Fitzgerald Publishing Co., 1974.

Black Man of the Nile, Yosef ben-Jochannan, Baltimore, Md.: Black Classic Press.

Sundiata: An Epic of Old Mali. D. T. Niane, London: Longman Group, Ltd., 1969.

 # The Middle Passage

Africans endured a harsh journey into slavery—from the West African coast across the Atlantic Ocean to the New World. Usually, they were taken to the Caribbean where some remained as slaves, while many others were shipped to North and South America. Historians refer to that journey as "the middle passage." From the moment of capture in their villages Africans suffered, and their suffering increased during the middle passage.

Some captains had the slaves branded with red-hot irons as soon as a trade was completed. This was done if the slaves were to be left ashore in the barracoons for any length of time. It prevented dishonest traders from substituting old or sickly slaves for the healthy ones already paid for. One captain noted that in the branding "care is taken that women, as the tenderest, be not burned too hard."

The Caribbean and South America

Many Africans who were enslaved on the Caribbean Islands and in South America did not forget their African culture, in spite of the cruel treatment they received and slave masters' attempts to stamp out the African way of life. Today African culture is clearly visible in Caribbean and South American music, food, dance, and folk literature—strong evidence of the resiliency of African culture. Perhaps you know people from Haiti, Brazil, Cuba, Jamaica, or Guyana. What do these different groups of people have in common? In what ways are they different?

FACTS

1. Many Africans fought against the onslaught of slave traders. Angola, led by Queen Nzingha, battled the Portuguese for over forty years.

2. Some African chiefs were encouraged by Europeans to capture and sell Africans into slavery.

3. The middle passage was the harsh voyage across the Atlantic Ocean to the New World.

4. The European slave trade began in the 1500's.

5. Slavery began in the Americas in the 1600's.

Investigate

- Slavery in the Caribbean and South America
- African Domestic Slavery
- Slavery in the United States

How were the three types of slavery alike?
How were they different?

RESOURCES

Before the Mayflower. Lerone Bennett, Chicago, Ill.: Johnson Publishing Co., 1982.

Black Patriot and Martyr, Toussaint of Haiti. Ann Griffiths. New York: Julian Messner.

They Came Before Columbus. Ivan Van Sertima. New York: Random House.

The Long Bondage, 1441–1815, James McCague. Champaign, Ill.: Garrard Publishing Co., 1972.

Activity: Acting It Out ✔

What Did It Feel Like to Be a Slave?

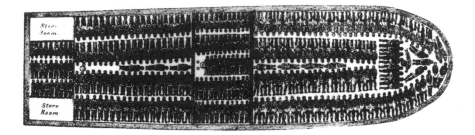

A diagram of a slave ship shows how Africans were crammed into the hull.

What did it feel like to be a slave? To be crowded in cramped living quarters on a ship? To experience, in a very minor way, the physical discomforts Africans endured during the middle passage, carry out the following activity.

Materials
- corrugated cardboard
- wide masking tape

Have at least three children or adults sit on the floor, one behind the other, with knees drawn up. Using corrugated cardboard and masking tape, build a shelter whose roof is horizontal and the length of the three participants. The width should be approximately three feet. The height of the shelter should be three feet, three inches.

Attach three pieces of cardboard to the roof to form the back and two side ends of the shelter. Leave open the front so that the rest of the class can see the participants.

Have the "slaves" remain in the shelter for approximately ten minutes or until they are uncomfortable. When the time is up, ask them to come out and share their feelings.

Communication: One language/Many languages

To keep slaves under control and to lessen the possibility of escape, slave traders encouraged slave masters to buy Africans who spoke different languages. Being unable to communicate ensured that slaves would not make plans to harm the slave masters and their families or to escape.

Such a strategy made it difficult for slaves to speak to one another, but before long they learned the language of the New World. The slaves' new language enabled them to do exactly what slave masters had tried to prevent—communication with other slaves.

Read About

Spirituals—What role did they play in the lives of slaves, and later, in the lives of post-slavery African-Americans?
Blues—How do they differ from spirituals? What role do both play now?
Campground Church Services—What freedom did they provide for the slave?

RESOURCES

To be A Slave. Julius Lester. New York: Dial, 1968.
Lay My Burden Down: A Folk History of Slavery. Benjamin Botkin (ed.). Atlanta: University of Georgia Press, 1989.
The Music of Black Americans—A History. Eileen Southern. New York: W. W. Norton, 1983.
Blues People, LeRoi Jones (Amiri Baraka). New York: William Morrow, 1963.
I'm Going to Sing; Black American Spirituals: Vol. II. Ashley Bryan. New York: Atheneum, 1982.

Photo Courtesy Africa Report.

Slavery vs. Freedom

The Amistad *Incident*

In 1839 Joseph Cinque, a young African from Sierra Leone, was kidnapped with other Africans and forced aboard a slave ship that sailed to Havana, Cuba. In Havana, Cinque and fifty-two other Africans were bought by a Spaniard. The young Africans were taken aboard a schooner, the *Amistad*, to be transported to the Spaniard's sugar plantation in Puerto Principe, Cuba.

Although in chains, Cinque did not lose hope. One night he and the other Africans escaped from their chains, seized weapons, and fought the ship's crew. Only two crew members survived the attack. Cinque told the survivors to sail back to Africa. But the crew members sailed to the United States where Cinque and the others were arrested.

A long court trial followed. During the trial Cinque spoke, through an interpreter, in defense of himself and his friends. Eventually the judge ruled in favor of the African and in 1842, Cinque and his friends returned to Africa.

FACTS

1. Cinque, the son of a Mendi Chief, was a great orator.

2. Cinque and his friends were *Bozales*, a term given to Africans newly arrived in Cuba.

3. In 1820 slavery was declared illegal in Spanish territories; thus Cinque and his friends were victims of an illegal trade.

4. Cinque's determination helped to win his freedom.

5. One of Cinque's lawyers was John Quincy Adams, a former United States president.

6. Martin Van Buren, U.S. president during Cinque's trial, was dissatisfied when the trial ended in favor of the Africans.

7. James Covey, a Mendi slave who spoke English, was Cinque's interpreter during the trial.

National Portrait Gallery, Smithsonian Institute

Joseph Cinque
1811–1879
birthplace—Sierra Leone
West Africa
"He Would Not Be A Slave"

FICTION

1. The *Amistad* was a ghost ship sailing along the Connecticut coast.

2. Cinque was a slave trader in Sierra Leone.

3. Cinque and the other Africans were *Ladinos*, a term given to Africans born or long settled in Cuba.

4. Once captured the Africans pretended not to understand English or Spanish.

RESOURCES

Afro-Bets Book of Black Heroes From A to Z. Wade Hudson and Valerie Wesley, Orange, N.J.: Just Us Books, 1988.

American Negro Slave Revolts. Herbert Aptheker. New York: International Publishers, 1983.

The Amistad Mutiny. Bernice Kohn, New York: The McCall Publishing Company, 1971.

From Slavery to Freedom: A History of American Negroes (4th Ed.). John Hope Franklin. New York: Knopf.

Activity: Stating Your Case
Persuasion vs.
Propaganda

Plan a Courtroom Debate

Form two teams with five participants on each team. The teams will debate the question "Should Africans Be Enslaved?" Encourage each team to use persuasive arguments in presenting their points of view. Use books from the suggestive reading list as well as others you may find in the library.

Investigate

- **Civil Disobedience**—When is it right to disobey a law? Hold a panel discussion to examine the pros and cons of civil disobedience.
- **Slave Revolts**—Some leaders: Denmark Vesey, Nat Turner, John Brown, Gabriel Prosser. Write and deliver a speech in defense of these men.
- **Abolitionists**—People who wanted to abolish slavery. Frederick Douglass, one of the most powerful abolitionists, said that the fourth of July was a cruel fraud for blacks living in the United States. Is Douglass' belief still true for today's African-Americans? Explain your answer.
- **Propaganda**—The repeated communication of ideas, information, or other material—often without regard to truth or fairness—for the purpose of winning people over to a belief or cause. What is the difference between persuasion and propaganda?
- **The Underground Railroad: Harriet Tubman**—Read about Moses, the biblical figure who led the Israelites out of Egypt. Why was Harriet Tubman called the "Moses of her people?" On a sheet of paper make two columns headed *Moses* and *Harriet Tubman*. List under each heading characteristics that describe the two figures.

Harriet Tubman
1826–1913
birthplace—Dorchester County, MD
"Black Moses"

Schomburg Center for Research in Black Culture

National Portrait Gallery, Smithsonian Institute

Frederick Douglass
1817–1895
birthplace—Talbot County, MD
"A Trumpet for Freedom"

THE MEANING OF JULY FOURTH FOR THE NEGRO

Speech at Rochester, New York, July 6, 1852

Fellow-citizens, pardon me, allow me to ask, why am I called upon to speak here to-day? What have I, or those I represent, to do with your national independence? Are the great principles of political freedom and of natural justice, embodied in that Declaration of Independence, extended to us? and am I, therefore, called upon to bring our humble offering to the national altar, and to confess the benefits and express devout gratitude for the blessings resulting from your independence to us? ... The rich inheritance of justice, liberty, prosperity and independence, bequeathed by your fathers, is shared by you, not by me. The sunlight that brought light and healing to you, has brought stripes and death to me. This Fourth July is yours, not mine. You may rejoice, I must mourn. To drag a man in fetters into the grand illuminated temple of liberty, and call upon him to join you in joyous anthems, were inhuman mockery and sacrilegious irony. Do you mean, citizens, to mock me, by asking me to speak today?

RESOURCES

Black Abolitionists. Benjamin Quarles. New York: Oxford University Press.

Great Negroes Past and Present. Russell Adams. Chicago: Afro-American Publishing Co., 1984.

The Black American: A Brief Documentary History. Leslie H. Fishel, Jr., and Benjamin Quarles. New York: Scott.

The Life and Times of Frederick Douglass, written by Himself. Frederick Douglass. Hartford, Conn.: Park Publishers, 1881. Abridged and reprinted. New York: Grosset & Dunlop, 1970.

The Oral Tradition

Preserving History

The oral tradition is an important aspect of African culture. It is also the basis of modern African literature. Tales handed down from one generation to the next teach people how to behave, explain occurrences in nature, and preserve historical facts. Preserving history in traditional African societies is the sole responsibility of *griots*, community historians, who begin their training as young men. With their agile minds, griots memorize countless historical facts and recite them while playing musical instruments. People in a community are entertained and at the same time they learn important lessons.

"Not through height does one see the moon."
Nigerian proverb

"The way water moves on the surface is not the way it moves on the bottom."
Liberian proverb

"When your hand is in Lion's mouth, be careful how you take it out."
Liberian Proverb

"De noise of de wheels don't measure de load in de wagon."
African-American proverb

Storytelling

Africans brought to the New World their tales and their love of storytelling. It was illegal for slaves to speak or write their own languages, and they were forbidden to read or write the language of the New World. So slaves told stories—especially animal tales. Brer' Rabbit became a cultural hero among slaves because of his cunning and ability to manipulate situations. Storytelling also helped to foster a feeling of unity among slaves, which helped them to endure hard times. Slave preachers used dramatic interpretations of Biblical stories to relay hope to the oppressed slaves. Much is to be said in favor of the power of spoken words.

Ain't I A Woman?

As opposition to the "peculiar institution" of slavery increased, great orators arose among the slaves in the United States. One of these orators was Sojourner Truth. She frequently responded to heckling men in audiences who wanted to deny women the equality of men. Her famous words, "Ain't I a woman?" spoken during her speech given at the 1852 Women's Rights Convention in Akron, Ohio united forever the causes of women's rights and the rights of black people.

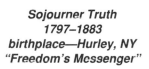

Sojourner Truth
1797–1883
birthplace—Hurley, NY
"Freedom's Messenger"

Look at my arm. I have ploughed and planted and gathered into barns, and no man could head me—and ain't I a woman? I could work as much and eat as much as any man—when I could get it—and bear the lash as well! And ain't I a woman? I have born thirteen children and seen most of 'em sold in slavery, and when I cried out with my mother's grief, none but Jesus heard me—and ain't I a woman?

—Sojourner Truth

Investigate

- **Speeches** by Malcolm X., Dr. Martin Luther King, Jr., Rev. Jesse Jackson, Rev. Adam Clayton Powell, former congresswomen Shirley Chisholm and Barbara Jordan. List common characteristics. What are the differences? Can you connect each to the oral tradition?

- **African-American Folktales**—Can you find the moral in each? Are there other hidden meanings?

The Power of Persuasion

Frederick Douglass was a 19th century contemporary of Sojourner Truth. He was a great orator who made fiery speeches against slavery. Later, the gift of oratory was exhibited by Marcus Garvey, Dr. Martin Luther King, Jr. and Malcolm X. Today we see that gift come forth in speeches made by Rev. Jesse Jackson, a recent candidate for the Democratic nomination for president.

Rap

Rap is a part of the African-American oral tradition. It is very popular with young African-Americans and is steadily becoming a part of the popular music scene. Rap is speech delivered with a strong rhythmic beat that is often accompanied by music, with a particular emphasis on the drum. Some songs deal with serious social issues. For example, "Self Destruction," recorded by an array of rappers under the name "Stop The Violence Movement" addressed the problem of black on black crime.

Individually, with a partner, or in a group, select a current social issue and create a rap about it. Perform your rap for an audience.

Malcolm X
1925–1965
birthplace—Omaha, NB
"Fighter for Freedom"

Schomburg Center for Research in Black Culture

Read About

The Oral Tradition—African and African-American. Read African and African-American tales. Select a tale and retell or dramatize it for an audience. Write and illustrate a tale of your own.

Marcus Garvey and his **"Back to Africa Movement".** How did Marcus Garvey persuade people to join his movement? How would you persuade your friends to leave the United States? How would you convince them to stay?

Jamaica—Marcus Garvey's birthplace. Learn about Jamaica and give a talk about the island. Use pictures and maps to make your talk exciting. What would Marcus Garvey think about Rastafarians? Is reggae music a form of rap? Why or why not?

Malcom X and **Dr. Martin Luther King, Jr.**—Why do you think they were able to influence so many people? How were they different from Marcus Garvey and Elijah Muhammad? What did they have in common?

RESOURCES

The Autobiography of Malcolm X, as told to Alex Haley, New York, 1966.

Lay My Burden Down: A Folk History of Slavery. Benjamin Botkin, (ed.). Atlanta: University of Georgia Press, 1989.

Speak to the Winds: Proverbs From Africa. Kofi Asare Opoku. New York: Lothrop, Lee and Shepard.

Talk that Talk: An Anthology of Afro-American Storytelling. Linda Goss and Marion E. Barnes. New York: Simon & Schuster, 1989.

The People Could Fly. Virginia Hamilton. New York: Alfred Knopf, 1985.

Why We Can't Wait. Martin Luther King, Jr., New York: New American Library, 1964.

Reconstruction to Civil Rights

(Harper's Weekly, Nov. 1867)

"The First Vote"

Reconstruction

Following the Civil War which ended in 1865, Congress passed several acts to help freed slaves make the transition from slavery to freedom. Among those passed were the *Freedmen's Bureau Act* and the *Civil Rights Act*, both aimed at assuring equality before the law for blacks. These acts were not solely benevolent, however. Newly freed slaves were often used as pawns in a battle for power between Republicans and Democrats. Another law, the *Reconstruction Act of 1867*, placed the South under temporary military occupation.

Protected by federal troops new governments in the South, headed by Republicans who garnered the support of recently enfranchised blacks and a sizeable white minority, established state laws that outlawed discrimination, instituted the first state-supported free public school systems and made labor laws fairer to employees. Many blacks were elected to local, state, and even federal offices. The *14th Amendment* (which essentially declared blacks citizens) and the *15th Amendment* (which enfranchised blacks) were ratified during this period that historians call "Reconstruction."

The Reconstruction period lasted from 1865 to 1877. It ended when Rutherford B. Hayes replaced Ulysses S. Grant as President and removed the troops. Once federal troops were removed, southern whites quickly seized control again. They terrorized blacks and passed laws that disenfranchised and relegated them to second class citizenship. Institutionalized racism became the rule and terms such as "separate but equal," "Jim Crow," and "grandfather clause" became a part of America's vocabulary.

Civil Rights

The years since the end of Reconstruction have seen a constant struggle for black equality and civil rights. That struggle has produced numerous victories that have helped make a fairer America. The *Brown vs. Board of Education of Topeka, Kansas* Supreme Court decision, the *Civil Rights Act of 1964,* the *Voting Rights Act* and the *Fair Housing Act* are just a few of those victories.

No one typifies the struggle for black equality better than Rosa Parks. She was the spark that lit the fire of the civil rights movement when she refused to give up her seat to a white man on a bus. The most important civil rights leader was Dr. Martin Luther King, Jr. who fanned the flames of the fire lit by Rosa Parks. Other important leaders during the civil rights movement included Malcolm X, Fannie Lou Hamer, Thurgood Marshall, Constance Baker Motley, Whitney Young, Daisy Bates, Roy Wilkins, Stokley Carmichael and Angela Davis.

Making Decisions/Doing the Right Thing

In Rosa Parks' eyes she was doing the right thing by refusing to give up her seat to a white person. In the eyes of southern white society, she committed a crime. Mrs. Parks made a decision that resulted in her arrest, but it was a decision that she has not regretted—and neither have African-Americans.

It is important to stand up for one's beliefs and one's rights. The consequences may be harsh for making decisions that go against society's rules, but there comes a time when such decisions must be made.

Martin Luther King, Jr.

Activity: Mobilizing a Movement

How to Organize a Protest

Do you have a complaint against society? How would you lodge your complaint and to whom? You may do so

(1) in a letter to a local government official.
(2) in a protest march.

Organize a protest march.
Remember to do the following:

1. *Gather people who have a similar complaint.*
2. *Choose a spokesperson.*
3. *Design placards that announce your complaint.*
4. *Choose a day for the march that is convenient to most of the protesters.*
5. *Advertise the march so that other interested people may join.*
6. *Choose a place where protesters may gather on the day of the march.*
7. *Choose a place where the march will end.*
8. *Design leaflets containing your complaint to hand out to people passing by.*

Investigate

- **Montgomery Bus Boycott, 1955–1956**
- **March on Washington, DC, 1963**
- **Selma-to-Montgomery March, 1965**
- **Affirmative Action**
- **Public School Busing**

Search old magazines and newspapers for pictures and articles about the civil rights activities above. Then search current magazines and newspapers for information on today's civil rights activities. Create a scrapbook entitled *Civil Rights: Then and Now.*

Read About

- **Montgomery, Alabama Bus Boycott,**—Why was it so important to the civil rights movement of the 1960's? If it had not occurred do you think the civil rights movement would have taken place? Explain your answer. What role did television play during this period?

- **Non-violence, Black power, Black Nationalism, Nation of Islam** and **Cultural Nationalism**—Describe each ideology and assess the role each played in the struggle for equality and self-determination.

RESOURCES

Reconstruction After the Civil War. John Hope Franklin. Chicago: University of Chicago Press, 1962.

The Trouble They Seen: Black People Tell the Story of Reconstruction Dorothy Sterling, (ed.). New York: Doubleday.

A Pictorial History of Blackamericans. Langston Hughes, Milton Meltzer, and C. Eric Lincoln. New York: Crown Publishers, Inc., 1956, 1963, 1968, 1973.

Don't Ride the Bus on Monday (The Story of Rosa Parks). Louise Meriwether. Englewood Cliffs, NJ: Prentice-Hall.

The Ballot or the Bullet, Malcolm X. (tape)
I Have a Dream, Martin Luther King, Jr. (tape)

Eyes on the Prize (movie & book)
Do the Right Thing (movie)
Mandela (videocassette)

The Diaspora

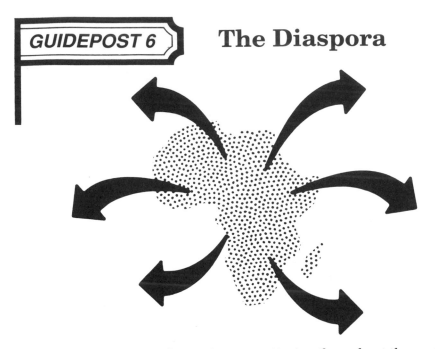

Diaspora means "a dispersion, or scattering throughout the world of a homogeneous people." The word originally referred to the dispersion of the Jews, after the capture of Babylon, throughout the Gentile world.

In the context of African history, the diaspora consists of people of African descent scattered throughout the world. Thus, black people on the Caribbean Islands, in South America, in the United States, in Great Britain, and in Europe are part of the African diaspora.

People of African descent have made invaluable contributions wherever they have lived or visited. An example was Paul Robeson, an artistic genius whose creative ability ranged from the football field, to the stage, to the concert hall and to the courtroom. No matter where life's paths led him, Paul Robeson encouraged people to end prejudice and oppression everywhere. His origins were African-American. His vision was global.

Making Connections

In the United States, the policy of "separate but equal" was a practice that had been legalized and reinforced by a Supreme Court decision in the *Plessey* vs. *Ferguson* case in 1896. It was the law of the land until decades of struggle brought it to an end (*Brown* vs *Board of Education of Topeka, Kansas*). Separate but equal is very similar to the policy of **apartheid** now employed in South Africa. This harsh system forces black South Africans to live, work, and be educated apart from white South Africans in unequal and often deplorable conditions. Like African Americans in the United States, black South Africans are struggling to liberate themselves from the horrors of apartheid. Anti-apartheid demonstrations occur daily in South Africa, and thousands of black South Africans have died in confrontations with the police and army.

Eliminating Racism

Racism is the belief and doctrine that one race is inherently superior to another and has the right to dominate and rule the race believed to be inferior. It may be practiced by individuals or by institutions.

The struggle for equality and self determination by Africans and people of African descent has been virtually worldwide. Whether in the Caribbean, South America, or in Europe, they have fought for decades to secure their rightful place among the world's nation of people.

The struggle to eliminate colonialism and oppression based primarily on race has fostered a bond among many people of African descent. "Africa" has become the rallying cry for them. And, for them, concepts such as "negritude," "Pan-Africanism," and "Back to Africa" express the importance of the African continent to the African diaspora. People such as W.E.B. DuBois, Marcus Garvey, Leopold Senghor, Malcolm X, and Archbishop Desmond Tutu have forced the world to see Africa in a different light. What Europeans once called the "dark continent" is now recognized as the birthplace of mankind and the "cradle of civilization."

Photo Courtesy Africa Report.

Activity: Talk It Out Putting It All Together

Imagine that Dr. Martin Luther King, Jr., a leader of the civil rights movement in the United States, and Archbishop Desmond Tutu, a leader of the anti-apartheid movement in South Africa, meet. Write the conversation you think might take place. What would these two leaders have in common? What advice do you think Dr. King could give to Archbishop Tutu?

Imagine you are living in a southern state during the 1890s. Write a letter to someone your age who is living in Soweto, South Africa. What would you have in common to share? What encouragement could you offer to your pen pal?

Imagine that you are Marcus Garvey. Convince a gathering of African Americans why they should return to Africa.

Read About

- **The struggle for independence in Africa**
- **The civil rights movement** in the United States
- **Self-determination** in the Caribbean and South America
  What do these three have in common? What makes each struggle different or unique?

Investigate

- **African-influenced cuisine.** Compile a list of dishes that may have been influenced by African cultures. Prepare some of the dishes and invite relatives and friends to sample them.
- **Haiti** (Santo Domingo) the first independent black country in the Western Hemisphere. Why was the rebellion there successful? What effect did it have on the slave systems in other countries in the Western Hemisphere?
- **Pan-Africanism**—Describe it. Who were some of its proponents? How does it relate to nationalism and self-determination?
- **Apartheid**—Describe it. Is there a relationship between Pan-Africanism and apartheid? Explain your answer.

The Africa News Cookbook: African Cooking for Western Kitchens. Tami Hultman. New York: Penguin Books, 1985.

African Roots in Britain. Mekada J. Alleyne. London, England: Kemet-Nubia Educational Materials, 1989.

Annie John. Jamaica Kincaid. New York: Farrar, Straus and Giroux, 1985.

Black Jacobins: Toussaint L'Ouverture and the San Domingo Revolution. Cyril R. James. New York: Random House, 1989.

Marcus Mosiah Garvey: Up You Mighty People, You Can Accomplish What You Will. Charles Barron. Brooklyn, NY: Dynamics of Leadership, Inc.

Looking at the Present

1. What are some of the problems facing African-Americans today? How can they be solved?
2. What are some of the problems facing people on the African continent? How can they be solved?
3. What role can all people play in helping to solve these problems?
4. Identify a problem and tell how you would solve it.

Investigate

• **Recent accomplishments of African-Americans** in politics, science, medicine, sports, education, entertainment, space exploration, etc. Choose five areas and write about the accomplishments of two African-Americans in each area.

• **Dr. Martin Luther King's dream**—What was it? How close is it to being realized? Describe the kind of world you would like to see.

Photo Courtesy Africa Report.

Using What You Have Learned

The following activities are excellent ways to culminate Black History Month Observances. They can also be used throughout the year. Each activity will be more meaningful after successfully completing the guideposts and activities on previous pages of this handbook.

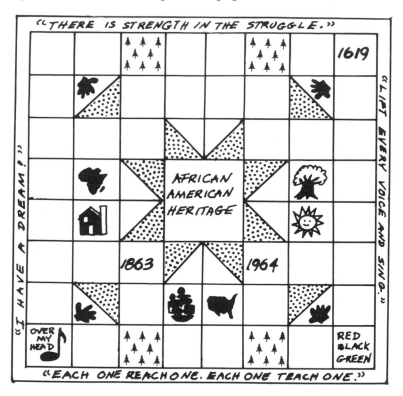

#1 Make a Heritage Quilt

When Africans came to America, they brought with them a history of working with textiles, spinning and weaving. Many of these skills were utilized during the plantation period and adapted to quilting techniques passed down from Europe.

Quilts as they are popularly known today, fall into two general groups—the "pieced work" and the "patchwork." In "pieced work," small scraps of cloth are sewn together to form a patterned top. In "patchwork" or "laid on" quilts, designs are appliqued onto a solid background. Tiny patches of cloth are turned under and stitched with little hemming stitches. This form of "applique" originated in Egypt. Similarly appliqued banners and wall hangings have long been made in Dahomey (now Benin), West Africa.

This handbook activity shows how traditional and modern techniques may be adapted in a hands-on group effort to create a visual centerpiece for the celebration of Black History Month. Other activities may be tied into this as well.

Materials: Enough **felt** to make sixty four (64) 12 × 12 inch squares in various colors. We suggest 1 yard (54 inches wide) each of red, yellow, blue and green; **scissors** (make sure they are sharp enough for cutting felt) and several **rulers**; **Elmer's glue**, a pack of large eye **needles**, **thread**, white **chalk**, **magic markers**, **crayons**, scraps of printed materials or **fabric** remnants from crafts or hobby stores, single sheets of 8-1/2 × 11 **paper**; a large **work table**.

Instructions:

1. Group the pre-cut squares by colors into separate piles. Let each participant select a patch to decorate and a sheet of paper for notes or sketches. Leave the other materials in a central location to be shared by everyone.

2. Measure 1/2 inch margins on each square and mark them off with chalk. Leave the margins free of design.

3. Have each participant select a theme for decorating his or her square.

Hint: The leader may put a list of general themes into a fishbowl or participants may select their own themes.

Examples: a quote or saying ("each one teach one"), a favorite subject (science/Benjamin Banneker), a hero (Harriet Tubman), a song (*Swing Low, Sweet Chariot*), a food (yam or peanut), an animal (tortoise or hare), or any symbols/image related to African-American culture.*

---

*Leaders may use the *Guideposts* in this book to stimulate participants' thoughts about themes for their individual patches. This activity may take several sessions to complete. Senior citizens may be asked to volunteer their recollections about traditional quilting bees. Older children may help younger ones with their designs. Group leaders are encouraged to adapt the materials available and to tailor the instructions to the age groups with which they are working. Participants may use music in the background for inspiration. In any case, the activity should be social and approached in a spirit of co-operation and entertainment. The finished product may be larger or smaller than described in the instructions depending on the number and involvement of participants.

4. Have each participant decorate his or her patch by cutting out shapes or letters from the scraps of materials. Glue the shapes to the patch and finish off the design with stitches, buttons, notions, or found items.

5. When each individual patch is completed (let patches set overnight to dry completely) stitch them together in eight vertical or horizontal strips. Using the reference materials below as a guide, arrange the patches in alternate patterns or colors. Later, stitch the eight strips together to make a quilt or a community wall hanging.

6. Have each participant describe his or her patch on a sheet of paper, identified by name, age, and date. Collect the descriptions into a group scrapbook. Donate the book to the next class or group to follow. Select a name for the book and quilt, i.e., *Our First African-American Heritage Quilt*.

7. Let each participant talk about the meaning of his or her patch at the end of the group activity (oral history). Make a recording or video tape of the reports.

8. Hang the Heritage Quilt in a prominent location in your class, church, or community center. Use it as a backdrop for an assembly program or another special event during Black History Month.

#2 Plan a Mini African-American Festival

This is an opportunity for your class or group to organize its own festival. Parents and children may participate. Projects developed by students in earlier units may be displayed. The mini festival may include anything related to the African and African-American experiences— food, storytelling, games, films, music, a play, a speech, dance. We suggest that the area used for the festival be decorated with posters and materials that reflect elements of the diaspora. Parents should be encouraged to assist in securing the decorations, preparing dishes, and helping to organize the festival. Participants may invite friends and relatives to the festival. Remember it is very important to capture the flavor of the African-American culture.

(all ages)

Ideas:

1. Let participants perform a dance routine to the music "The Greatest Love of All."

2. With a mixed group of no more than fifteen people play the whispering game, "Pass It On." This game illustrates oral communication. Note how information changes as it's passed on by word of mouth. Allow the last person in the group to relate the information to a designated reporter who will write about the "story."

3. Sing a Song. Reproduce the lyrics to the song, **Lift Evr'y Voice and Sing**. Sing it at the beginning of your celebration.

4. Perform an original rap to illustrate a theme from African-American history.

5. Perform a play.

6. Display original paintings, crafts, books, and art work.

#3 Write a Family History

Encourage participants to write about their family history. Each participant should talk with family members to record facts as well as colorful anecdotes.

(all ages)

#4 Construct a Black Heroes Scrapbook

Each participant should be encouraged to collect photographs of important heroes of African descent. The heroes may or may not be well known. Participants should cut magazine and newspaper photographs and paste them onto construction paper. Family photos may also be used. Encourage participants to write on the paper the hero's name as well as a brief statement about the person's contributions. Collect all the paste-ups and staple them into book format..

(pre-K and early readers)

#5 Create a Collage or a Wall Mural

Create a collage or a group mural. Use a roll of brown wrapping paper (about 15 to 20 feet long) and tape it to a wall in your school or community center. Instruct each participant to illustrate some significant event in African-American history. Color with crayons or markers; paste on clippings from old newspapers, and pictures from magazines. Each participant's section should not exceed the width of one and one half feet. Display the mural in an appropriate place. If brown wrapping paper is not available let each participant design a poster depicting his or her own expression of the Black History Month Observance.

(pre-K and up)

#6 Spotlight a Real Life Experience

Perhaps there is a parent or some individual from the community who has first-hand knowledge of some of the areas covered in this book. For example, there are some parents or grandparents who lived in the South and experienced segregation and Jim Crow laws. Invite them to talk about their experiences. Supplement their talk with video presentations. Perhaps there are other parents from the African diaspora who were born and raised in the Caribbean or in South America. Invite them to talk about their country and to tell how its culture differs from African-American culture in the United States.

(all ages)

RESOURCES

The Patchwork Quilt by Valerie Flournoy. New York: Dial, 1985.
African Crafts by Jane Kerina, New York: The Lion Press, 1970.
Transformations, A Rites of Passage Manual for African-American Girls. Gilyard, Moore, King and Warfiled-Coppock, New York: Stars Press, 1987.

Questions and Answers

No doubt this handbook will raise just as many questions as it answers. Take a look at page 5 (**A Quick Quiz**). If you have not already done so, complete the crossword puzzle. The answers appear below. The true/false answers for page 6 are also shown. Now try to answer the questions on this page. If necessary, refer to the pages indicated in parentheses to refresh your memory.

¹R	O	S	A	²P	A	R	K	S		³S	
E				U						E	
⁴C	I	V	I	L			⁵P	A	U	L	
O			⁶L	O	⁷V	E				M	
N		ˣD		R		⁹A	R	I	A		
¹⁰S	H	O	E		A		N				
T		U		¹¹T	¹²R	U	T	H			
¹³R	U	G	¹⁴P	O	E	T			¹⁵G		
U		¹⁶L	¹⁷A		R				R		
¹⁸C		A	M	I	S	T	A	¹⁹D		I	
T		S					²⁰A	²¹R	E		
I		²²S	²³O	J	²⁴O	U	R	N	E	R	
²⁵O	²⁶N				N				N		
²⁷N	A	T		²⁸V	E	S	E	Y			

T 1.
F 2.
T 3.
T 4.
F 5.
F 6.
F 7.
T 8.
F 9.

I. Africa—The Beginning (6–11)

1. Name three (3) major African kingdoms. Explain their importance.
2. Name four powerful ancient African leaders.
3. Why is Africa referred to as the birthplace of mankind?

II. The Middle Passage (12–15)

1. What was the middle passage?
2. Did slavery in the United States differ from slavery in other parts of the world? Explain your answer.
3. What countries played significant roles in the slave trade?

III. Slavery vs. Freedom (16–19)

1. Who was Gabriel Prosser and why is he important?
2. Who was Denmark Vesey? What made his ideas significant?
3. Name some prominent abolitionists. What role did they play in the struggle to end slavery?

IV. The Oral Tradition (20–23)

1. What relation does Sojourner Truth have to the abolitionist and suffrage movements?
2. Why did slaves consider Brer Rabbit tales edifying?
3. Why have black ministers been traditionally at the forefront of the anti-slavery and civil rights movements?

V. Reconstruction to Civil Rights (24–27)

1. What is civil disobedience?
2. Who was the mother of the civil rights movement?
3. Why is the NAACP important to the civil rights movement? What other organizations are important?

VI. The Diaspora (28–31)

1. How were Paul Robeson's actions related to the concept of diaspora?
2. Who is Nelson Mandela and why is he important?
3. List several ideas these thinkers had in common: W.E.B. DuBois, Marcus Garvey, Malcolm X, Martin Luther King, Jr., Archbishop Desmond Tutu.
4. Define racism in your own words.
5. What does the notion of brotherhood mean to you?

A Note for Teachers

A great deal has been published about the African-American experience, and much of that material is excellent. New research is being published daily, and many schools have begun to recognize the importance of the study of African history and the value of infusing within the curriculum African and African-American content. Space does not permit the evaluation of all the material currently available, but included in this handbook are some sources that may be useful to teachers and families. Upon written request, distributors and wholesalers may provide more complete bibliographies of their materials.

In her book *Black Focus on MultiCultural Education*, Beryle Banfield suggests excellent criteria for selecting instructional materials, analyzing them, and establishing positive practices for anti-racist and anti-sexist classrooms. This book is highly recommended for those who are serious about fair and unbiased teaching of African-American history and culture.

Black Focus on MultiCultural Education: How to Develop an Anti-Racist, Anti-Sexist Curriculum. Beryle Banfield, New York: Edward Blyden Press, 1979.

More Resources

The following sources focus or specialize in materials or programs dealing with the African-American experience.

To expedite your inquiries to small presses, publishers and book distributors, please be sure to enclose a self-addressed, stamped (45¢) business size envelope for the return of ordering information.

BOOKS

Adventures in Reading, 1525 E. 53d St., Suite 901, Chicago, Ill. 60615.

Africa World/Red Sea Press, 15 Industry Court, Trenton, N.J. 08638.

African-American Images, c/o Jawanza Kunjufu, Chicago, Ill.

Afro-American Distributors, 53 W. Jackson Blvd. #1040, Chicago, Ill. 60604.

Alkebulan Images, 2721 Jefferson St., Nashville, TN 37208.

The Black Book Club, c/o Norrine Dunnevile, 215 North Ave. West, Westfield, NJ 07090.

Black Butterfly/An imprint of Writers and Readers Press, 210 West 137th Street, New York, N.Y. 10030.

Black Classic Press, P.O. Box 13414, Baltimore, MD 21203.

The Council on Interracial Books for Children, 1841 Broadway, New York, NY 10023.

Winston Derek Distributors, 17-22 West End Ave., Nashville, Tenn. 37203.

ECA Associates, P.O. Box 15004 Great Bridge Station, Chesapeake, Va. 23320.

Johnson Publishing Co, 1821 S. Michigan Ave., Chicago, Ill. 60616.

Just Us Books, Inc. 301 Main St. #22-24, Orange, N.J. 07050.

Kitchen Table: Women of Color Press, P.O. Box 908, Latham, N.Y. 12110.

Luchena Books, 229-21B Merrick Blvd, Laurelton, N.Y. 11413.

New Day Press/KARAMU, 2355 East 89th Street, Cleveland, Ohio 44106.

Open Hand Press, 600 E. Pine, Suite 565, Seattle, Wash. 98122.

Roger Robbie Creations, P.O. Box 5657, Philadelphia, Penna. 19129

Sabayt Publications, 5441 S. Kenwood Ave., Chicago, Ill. 60615.

Third World Press, P.O. Box 730, 7524 S. Cottage Grove Ave., Chicago, Ill. 60619.

Warner Books, 114-36 Francis Lewis Blvd., Cambria Hts., N.Y. 11411.

BROADCAST MEDIA

(Check your local TV listings and cable channels for public affairs programming of interest during Black History Month.)

Black Entertainment TV
National Public Broadcasting System (PBS)   Ebony/Jet Showcase
Tony Brown's Journal   Essence TV

*BlacCast Entertainment (Black Films & Videos) 199-19 Linden Blvd., St. Albans, NY 11412.

CONFERENCES AND ORGANIZATIONS

National Black Child Development Conference, 1463 Rhode Island Ave., NW, Washington, DC 20005.

African-American Institute, UN Plaza, New York, NY

TransAfrica, 1325 18th Street, NW, Suite 202, Washington, DC 20036.

Caribbean Cultural Center, 408 West 58th Street, New York, NY 10019.

MultiCultural Publishers Exchange, P.O. Box 9869, Madison, WI 53715

FESTIVALS

Each year African-American festivals are sponsored by cities and municipalities throughout the country. Check your local chamber of commerce for dates and details.

PEOPLE

Brother Blue (storyteller) c/o Dr. Hugh Morgan Hill, 30 Fernald Drive, Cambridge, MA 02138.
Linda Goss (storyteller) c/o Hola Kumba Ya Productions, Dept. L88, 7125 Sprague St., Philadelphia, PA 19119.

PERIODICALS

(Check your local library for the latest regional and other African-American special interest publications. Lists of Afro-centric newspapers may also be found at the reference desk of your public library.)

American Visions Magazine
Black Enterprise
EBONY
Essence Magazine
Emerge Magazine
Jet
Journal of African Civilizations
Journal of Negro History
Harambee, a Newspaper for Young Readers (Just Us Books)

PLACES OF INTEREST

(Check your local arts council or chamber of commerce for galleries or museums in your area.)

Afro-American Historical and Cultural Museum, 7th & Arch Streets, Philadelphia, PA 19106.
Museum of National Center for Afro-American Artists, 300 Walnut Street, Roxbury, MA 02119.
National Afro-American Museum and Cultural Center, PO Box 578, Wilberforce, OH 45384.
National Museum of African Art/Smithsonian Institute, Washington, DC.
The Schomburg Center for Research in Black Culture, New York Public Library.
The Studio Museum in Harlem, 144 West 125th Street, New York, NY 10027.

PROGRAMS

Black Culture on Tour in America, c/o The Carter G. Woodson Foundation, PO Box 1025, Newark, NJ 07101.

SPECIAL EVENTS

January 15   Martin Luther King, Jr., Holiday Observed
December 26–January 1   Kwanzaa Observed

STORYTELLERS

National Association for the Preservation and Perpetuation of Storytelling (NAPPS). PO Box 309, Jonesborough, TN 37659 (Jackie Torrence)

Important Dates in African-American History

1565:   Black explorers accompany Spanish explorer Pedro Menéndez de Avilés during founding of St. Augustine, Florida.

1619:   Twenty Africans arrive in Jamestown, Virginia and become first slaves in North America.

1663:   Slaves and white indentured servants plan a rebellion in Gloucester County, Virginia.

1731:   Benjamin Banneker, inventor and scientist, is born November 9.

1746:   Toussaint L'Ouverture, revolutionary leader of Haiti, is born May 20.

1770:   Crispus Attucks is first to die in Boston Massacre (during Revolutionary War).

1773:   Chicago is founded by Jean Baptiste Pointe du Sable, black pioneer from Haiti.

1787:   Sojourner Truth, abolitionist and former slave, is born November 18.

1794:   African Methodist Episcopal denomination is founded in Philadelphia by Rev. Richard Allen.

1807:   United States Congress bans importation of slaves. British parliament abolishes slave trade.

1820:   First United States blacks arrive in Liberia, West Africa. United States Congress enacts Missouri Compromise, forbidding slavery north of Missouri.

1822:   Denmark Vesey's planned slave revolt is uncovered in Charleston, South Carolina. Thirty-seven blacks, including Vesey, are executed.

1827:   *Freedom's Journal*, first black newspaper, is published.

1831:   Nat Turner's slave uprising takes place. Fifty-five whites are killed before rebels are caught. Nat Turner is hanged.

1834:   Slavery is abolished throughout the British Empire.

1841:   United States Supreme Court declares freedom for slaves who revolted aboard the ship *Amistad* and orders their return to Africa.

1847:   Frederick Douglass publishes first issue of *North Star*.

1854:   Lincoln University, the first black college, is founded as Ashmun Institute in Chester County, Pennsylvania.

1857:   United States Supreme Court rules against Dred Scott (who has been residing in Minnesota, a free territory) and returns him to slavery.

1863:   President Abraham Lincoln issues the Emancipation Proclamation.

1865:   United States Congress passes 13th Amendment, abolishing slavery in the United States.

1870:   15th Amendment, giving blacks the right to vote, is ratified by United States Congress.

1873:   Slavery is abolished in Puerto Rico.

1883:   Jan Matzeliger patents shoe-lasting machine.

1888:	Slavery is abolished in Brazil.
	First black bank, Capitol Savings Bank of Washington, D.C., opens.
1893:	Dr. Daniel Hale Williams performs first successful open heart surgery.
1909:	NAACP is founded.
1913:	Rosa Parks is born February 4.
	Harriet Tubman, Underground Railroad "conductor", dies.
1916:	*Journal of Negro History* is first published.
1923:	Garrett A. Morgan patents traffic light.
1926:	Dr. Carter G. Woodson begins Negro History Week.
1948:	United States Supreme Court decision gives blacks the right to study law at state institutions.
1950:	Gwendolyn Brooks wins Pulitzer Prize for poetry.
1953:	United States Supreme Court ruling bans segregation in Washington, D.C. restaurants.
1955:	Marian Anderson debuts as first black singer at Metropolitan Opera House.
	Rosa Parks is arrested in Montgomery, Alabama for refusing to give her bus seat to a white man.
1957:	United States Congress passes Civil Rights Act. Nine children integrate Central High School in Little Rock, Arkansas.
	Ghana, first British colonial territory, becomes an independent African nation.
1960:	Four North Carolina A&T students begin Sit-in Movement in Greensboro. Sharpeville Massacre occurs in South Africa. Over sixty persons killed.
1962:	Nelson Mandela, South African freedom fighter, is imprisoned.
1963:	Medgar W. Evers, civil rights leader, is assassinated in Jackson, Mississippi.
	Four black girls are killed in Birmingham, Alabama church bombing.
	Dr. Martin Luther King, Jr. leads march on Washington, D.C., largest civil rights demonstration.
1964:	Dr. Martin Luther King, Jr. wins Nobel Peace Prize.
1966:	Edward W. Brooke becomes first black United States senator since Reconstruction.
1968:	Dr. Martin Luther King, Jr. is assassinated April 4.
1976:	Soweto uprising in South Africa. 200 unarmed schoolchildren are killed.
1983:	Lt. Col. Guion S. Bluford, Jr. becomes first black astronaut in space.
1986:	Dr. Martin Luther King, Jr.'s birthday (January 15) is celebrated as a legal national holiday in the United States.
1990:	Nelson Mandela is released (February 11) after more than 27 years in prison. He makes historic visit to the United States in June.

BLACK HISTORY CERTIFICATE

This certificate recognizes the commitment that _____ has made to learn more about the accomplishments and achievements of African-Americans.

DATE _____

signed _____